RISE AND SHINE

Inspirational Stories of Five Masters of Real Estate

FEATURING:

Dr. Masoud Abdar Esfahani, Nima Hessami,

Maryam Jalilalghadr, Stephen Katz,

Hamidreza Saeedabadi

Foreword by:
Kundan Joshi, Founder & CEO of TheAppLabb;
EY Entrepreneur of Year;
Top 150 Extraordinary Canadians

RISE AND SHINE: Inspirational Stories of Five Masters of Real Estate

Cover Design by Smart Shot

Published by North Star Success Inc.

🌐 www.northstarsuccess.com

✉ support@northstarsuccess.com

📞 +1 647 479 0790

Contents:

RISE AND SHINE

Inspirational Stories of Five Masters of Real Estate

Foreword by Kundan Joshi

When I started the business, I was a new immigrant, who had recently graduated, with no experience, no access to capital, no credit history, no cash, no savings, no network, no partners, no investors, with student debt to repay, with a family to support. But if I had focused on what I didn't have, I would have never been able to launch my business, a far cry from making it successful. I instead decided to focus on what I had - my goals and my strengths. I knew that I loved to take on challenges, I had energy, enthusiasm and a burning desire to make a big positive impact in the world. I loved technology and innovation, and I was passionate about helping people. I knew that I had always thrived under challenges and pressure; so I took them in my stride, while staying focused on my goals.

After graduating from engineering school at Western University, I worked as a software engineer during the day, and worked on my business at nights for many years, kept expanding my network; kept learning to accumulate skills and industry expertise, till I had finally saved enough. That's when I became a full-time entrepreneur from a what was initially a side hustle.

I had to bootstrap the business. I put together a talented team – one employee at a time, kept growing - one client at a time, kept scaling - one product at a time, built the brand - one successful project at a time.

There was no shortage of challenges in the journey. From failed partnerships to loss of revenue. But what helped me was the acknowledgement that I cannot win, if I don't fail. Its good to observe and learn from other's failures, but sometimes we need to lose to find our way. We need to fail to truly realize what needs to be fixed; to realize that we can't get comfortable in where we are, but we always need to push our boundaries, beyond our comfort zone, to strive to get to the next level. I always had belief in myself and the One above, that no matter how bad it gets, I will survive. No matter how deep I fall, I will rise. The never give up attitude, the grit and resilience to keep going, to keep plowing, to keep running.

And to stay positive, to look at the glass half full, its essential to focus our attention and energy from what we don't have, to what we have. To truly express our gratitude for everyone that has stood by us, regardless of whether things were good or bad. I have been truly blessed to have a loving and supportive family, who never stopped believing in me; partners, advisors and mentors who have always inspired and encouraged me to be a better leader. To employees who stood by my side, and to clients who placed their trust in me. I owe my success to them.

Kundan Joshi

Founder & CEO of TheAppLabb; EY Entrepreneur of Year; Top 150 Extraordinary Canadians

"Committed to Excellence"

Dr. Masoud Abdar Esfahani

Dr. Masoud Abdar Esfahani

Real Estate Professional

This is the story of a medical doctor who traveled halfway around the world to eventually become a real estate professional, now taking immense pride in delivering 5-star service to clients and continuing to dream big about what the future holds.

Jumping Out of Rehab

I'm a medical doctor by training, but after moving to Canada, I started working as a registered acupuncturist. In 2013 I partnered with a few of my friends to open a rehab center in Richmond Hill, Ontario, called ActivePro Health Clinic, and I worked there until 2015. In that year, one of our key partners who attracted a lot of the clientele decided to move back to his country of origin. During the same period of time, the other partners and I noticed the huge growth potential in the Canadian real estate market. Since I, personally, had a solid background in construction from back home in Iran (more on this below), we decided to close the clinic and pursue a new business endeavor in the construction industry.

This decision did not come easily, as I had other choices on the table at the time. First, I reconsidered getting my license as a medical doctor to begin practicing in Canada. However, deep down, I knew I was not meant to be a physician. I experienced the pain of going through medical school in Iran against my will, and I was sure I didn't want to endure the same torture another time. A second option was to focus on the other business that I was doing on the side. This work involved some international trade between China and Dubai, selling Chinese goods to my clients in Dubai. Unfortunately, this option didn't seem to be feasible either. Most of my customers in Dubai had sold their merchandise to Iran, and because of the unstable dollar-rial exchange rate and the ever-changing oil price in 2015, many of them stopped doing business with Iran. Clearly, going down that path was like beating a dead horse.

My strong background in construction came from working many years in the real estate industry as a project manager for our family business. The business had built and developed lots of projects in Iran, so we were quite well-known for our high-end mid-rise buildings. This background, in addition to my partners' and my belief that Canadian real estate was a good market in which to invest, led to our joint decision to start a property investment business in Toronto. According to our calculations at the time, building and selling a single luxury custom home in uptown Toronto could bring in an average profit of $200-300k for the investors. That didn't even include the potential additional profit due to land appreciation! Land prices in 2015 were going up by the second, and the real estate business was booming in Toronto. We took the plunge.

The Property Investment Rollercoaster

My partners and I started researching and interviewing several realtors whom we thought could help us find a suitable property to buy, demolish, build, and sell. That experience showed me one shocking trend: Most realtors aimed to earn a commission, not to assist their clients in making the best decision. I realized some realtors would even hide critical issues of a property from the potential buyer, just to make a quick buck. For example, one time my business partners and I were very close to making a firm offer to purchase a property which housed a huge but hidden problem. A large number of trees surrounding the property would need to be cut down in order for the city to permit us to build a custom home in this place. None of the realtors informed us we would eventually pay tens of thousands of dollars to remove those trees, but fortunately a friend of mine warned us of the issue and saved us from making that terrible mistake.

In the end, we decided not to hire a realtor to help us with our purchase at all. We chose to do this work for ourselves. Soon, we found a good property in one of the best neighborhoods in Toronto. We contacted the listing agent directly, struck a deal with the seller, and bought the property at a great price. We hired someone to demolish the old residence and build the custom home for us, and my partners picked me as the trusted representative who would oversee the project from start to finish.

During this first project I learned a lot, because the way construction is done in Canada is completely different from what I knew from Iran. The project took fifteen months to finish, and eventually we sold the home at a good profit. At that time, the real estate market remained reliable, and the property prices continued rising at a crazy pace. We figured it was no longer worthwhile to build custom homes for sale. We reasoned, "If we just buy and hold, the land appreciation rate is so high that we don't actually need to invest in building a luxury home on the property. The flipping process is extremely profitable in and of itself."

In the meantime, we decided to invest in other properties as well, and we hired a realtor to hunt for us. However, not all of our endeavors went as planned. We ran into a huge problem while closing on one of the properties in mid-2016. Fewer than 30 days before the closing, we realized there was an easement on the title of the property. Our real estate agent hadn't done a title search ahead of time, assuming there would be no issues, and therefore missed the easement clause. Since the deal was firm, we had no way out and had to close on it. We tried to rectify the problem to the best of our ability, but naturally we endured tremendous pressure and stress throughout the process.

This incident truly impacted my mentality, because not only did my partners indirectly blame me for all that went wrong (they put their trust in me and considered me accountable), but I also began to tell myself, "If I want to make it big in construction in Toronto, I need to know the ins and outs of the real estate market." I decided I was not going to risk trusting an inexperienced agent again; neither was I going to endanger my partners' trust in me another time. I felt a real need to take control and learn as much as I could about the real estate market. For these reasons, I enrolled in the courses offered by OREA (Ontario Real Estate Association) in September 2016, and by early 2017, I was a licensed realtor in Toronto.

Art of Facial Rejuvenation

While still involved in property investment with my partners, I began managing another business in the cosmetic industry. In March 2016, a few doctors and investors approached me and asked me to partner up with them to open and direct a beauty clinic in North York. Since I was formerly an MD and had the experience of working in the rehab center from 2013-2015, I was obviously a perfect fit for the position. Thus, 'Art of Facial Rejuvenation' was born. The property investment venture slowed down for a time, due to the bitter closing experience mentioned earlier, leaving me with ample time on my hands. Therefore, I devoted a large part of my time and energy to running and scaling the beauty clinic practice.

Growing More Serious as a Real Estate Professional

Initially, I didn't intend to become a full-time realtor. I merely signed up for the courses, because I wanted to make informed decisions for our team about what property to buy and what not to buy. However, I found myself buying a property for a friend after only a few months. My friend, a newcomer to Canada, entrusted me with his money, and I found a nice property for him in a great location. He was so pleased with the experience that one day he came to the beauty clinic in the middle of the day, hugged me in front of my staff, and while crying his eyes out, he told me, "Being an immigrant has been a really daunting task for me and my family. It has not been easy, but at least you made my most important investment go smoothly. I'm very happy that you were there to help me navigate the purchase of my home. I'd never seen such a caring and dedicated agent."

That interaction was a pivotal moment for me. I discovered how instrumental the services of a quality realtor can be, and I realized how much I loved being in the position of helping others make an informed choice and a wise purchase. That single experience made me more determined to pursue a career as a real estate agent.

Note: It's always been in me to give. It's always been in me to care. My clients often tell me that one of my key characteristics is patience. Once, I took a client of mine to 117 showings before they finally decided to buy! That specific client did not live in Toronto but wanted to buy a property in the city, so I sometimes went to showings on my own, took videos of the property, and sent the videos to him via WhatsApp. I attended some showings with the client, others with his wife, but rarely with both present. This client's wife once said to me, "You are so unusually patient. Any other realtor would have killed us when we asked to see one more property, but you were always on our side. Always present. Always helpful." I love helping people, no matter what. The smile on their faces means the world to me.

Things Getting Complicated

When the beauty clinic first opened in March 2016, I wrote a business plan and projected that we would break even in two years, and after that we could return a profit. Exactly at the second year mark, in March 2018, 'Art of Facial Rejuvenation' reached this break-even point and started to turn a profit. We even began thinking about franchising the practice. Business was great for a couple more months, until we encountered a real problem in May 2018. At the time, more than 80 percent of the clinic clients were Persian immigrants, not yet fully established in Canada, and to some extent dependent on money coming their way from back home. The economic turmoil in Iran disrupted the dollar-rial exchange rate to such an extent that our services were no longer affordable for those clients. The business went into the red and started losing money. My partners directed complaints to me, because I was the director and had told them the business would be profitable in 2018. They kept telling me, "We haven't been making any money for the past two years. How much more do you want us to pay out of our pockets in the hope of making profits in some unknown future?"

It was unfair. I delivered on my promise to break even in 2018, and we even started expanding the business to new locations. As the director and mastermind behind the business, I carried most of the workload, and I still split the profit with my partners. Despite all of this, the moment we started losing money, they claimed, "It's your fault. You don't know what you're doing."

During the same time period, I became better established as a realtor and secured many more deals. I achieved awards as a High Achievement agent as well as a Premier Club Member while doing real estate on a part-time basis. At this point, I informed my partners I would work at the clinic part-time from then on, and the other partners needed to put in their time and energy just like I had. I thought, "If this is a partnership, we need to be partners in everything. We should be sharing not only the profits, but also the responsibilities."

Calling it Quits

My client base in the real estate business continued to grow. I now had much more time available to focus on my business as a realtor and to increase my transactions. However, I faced a dilemma: the more marketing I did, the more prospects I had, and the more prospects I had, the more questions they asked me. I generally handle confusing questions by responding, "I don't know. Let me get back to you." However, my clients asked a good number of questions that I didn't know the answer to. I preferred not to face this situation in my work. I soon realized that one can't become a truly knowledgeable realtor just by taking the limited required courses and reading the few suggested books. I needed to learn more. True success required taking supplementary courses, going to seminars, studying a lot more, and keeping myself updated all the time. I aim for excellence in whatever I do and want to deliver the most comprehensive service to my clients. I have never merely "winged it" when it comes to business. Rather, I have always been committed to excellence.

One day in December 2018, I got into a heated argument with my partners at the beauty clinic. They told me, "You cannot manage this business profitably. We can do better ourselves." I replied simply, "OK. Take it away. It's all yours."

I gradually stepped away from the business, and eventually in February 2019, I quit. This was an emotionally challenging and sad decision, yet I was convinced it was for the best.

After leaving 'Art of Facial,' I had two good options left on the table: One was to dive back into the property investment business, still inactive after the Toronto real estate market crash in 2017. The other option involved going "all in" on the real estate agent business, which appealed to me in many ways. I saw myself creating tremendous value for my clients and making them happy through my services. Becoming a full-time realtor also meant that I would create a business just for myself, without partners who could dump their responsibilities on me or take away part of my profits.

In February 2019, I held an event, invited the key people in my network, and officially announced that I was thereafter a real estate agent and no longer committed to the beauty clinic. I let everybody know that I was ready to help with whatever real estate needs they might have.

The Proud Realtor

Up until then, I hesitated to introduce myself as a real estate professional at networking events. My hesitation might have come from hearing others say, "You were a medical doctor in Iran. It's below you to be in sales." However, I think if I'm serving my clients well, and if I'm doing a great job of solving their problems and getting them closer to their goals, then being a realtor is the most valuable and prestigious career ever. The greatest reward I get from this work is hearing from clients that I have managed to surpass their expectations.

I now proudly introduce myself as a real estate professional whose clients are extremely satisfied with his services. I encourage you, reader, to go to my website and read the incredible testimonials my clients have shared. Have a look at one of them below:

One of the hardest and stressful things in life is moving to a new place to live. It's very hard in Iran and even much harder in Canada. This is where a person needs a reliable and compassionate person for consultation and guidance. Someone who first thinks about you and your benefits, then think about their own business. Someone who is never tired of your objections, someone who you feel comfortable with and has a great network. If a problem arises in the middle of the deal, they will solve it because they know everything from A to Z. Thank god that we had one of the great realtors in Toronto Mr. Masoud Abdar Esfahani and his amazing team, Futurist home Group.

The past couple of years have been amazingly successful for me. I have won numerous awards as a top-producing agent and also earned the following certifications:

- 5-Star High Standard Real Estate Broker
- Accredited Buyer Representative
- Seller Representative Specialist
- CLHMS (Certified Luxury Home Marketing Specialist)
- International Property Specialist

My current goal is to start my own brokerage where I could have a team of realtors working for me. To accomplish this, I'm constantly investing in training and designations to prepare me for future roles and responsibilities. My ultimate plan is to establish a holding company that would assist with most challenges faced by first-time home buyers in Canada. Newcomers suffer terrible losses every single day, simply because they don't know many things about their new home country, and they trust unqualified service providers to assist them in the beginning. My holding company could provide a newcomer with the correct:

- realtor
- mortgage agent
- lawyer
- insurance agent

- property development department
- construction department
- renovation company
- advertising agency
- investment consultant
- business consultant

I have learned along my journey that everything you do is a valuable experience. Each person you meet can be your teacher; you only need to keep your eyes open. Whatever you go through, even that which doesn't turn out the way you wanted, adds to your pool of knowledge and experience. When people ask me, "Wasn't it a waste of time working in that beauty clinic for two years without turning any profit?" I reply, "Of course it wasn't a waste of time. A large part of my client base today came from the time I worked at the clinic. If you know how to look at experiences, you will believe as I do: nothing at all is wasted!"

Also, I'd like to emphasize resilience. Everybody gets knocked down at some point in life. And yes, of course it hurts to get beaten up. However, the important thing is to get back up as fast as you can and get back on track.

Time is precious, so don't waste it regretting what has gone wrong or could have been different.

Two Final Tips for Anyone Looking to Hire a Realtor

1. Hire the right person. Even if someone is introduced to you via referral, do your due diligence. Interview not only those referred to you, but also other professionals who might be able to help you. Check their knowledge, background, experience, and history. When you hire the proper agent, they will find the right property/location/buyer/seller for you at a fair price.

2. Be clear about what you can tolerate. If you're a buyer, don't get too hyped about the profits you could make if you take big risks. If you're a seller, be truthful about your numbers. By all means, take a risk, but make it a calculated one.

Committed

to Excellence

Author's Bio

Dr. Masoud Abdar Esfahani

is the founder of the Futurist Home Real Estate Team. He is a certified real estate broker, certified luxury home marketing specialist, certified buyer and seller representative specialist and international property specialist. As a full-time real estate professional, he has deep commitment to excellence. His mission is to provide the best possible service to help his clients throughout the entire process of purchasing their first home and beyond. He helps clients all over the GTA sell, buy, build, renovate, or do just about anything with their home. He strives to be the trusted knowledgeable source for his clients. As a high touch real estate team, Futurist Home is known for their extensive market knowledge and devotion to their clients.

Masoud's intention is always to use his strong negotiation skills that he's developed throughout his 30 years of experience across various industries in six different countries to the benefit of his clients. He is always there to get his clients exactly what they want and relieve them from the all the stresses that come with buying a home. Also, through his professional network of mortgage brokers, lawyers, marketers, and so on, he aims to make the process and transaction stress free.

He stays up-to-date with all the information and designations in the market to make sure his clients make the best decision whether they are buying, selling, or renting.

He is a Medical Doctor by education, but he has a long history of building different businesses from scratch and expanding them to large scales. With over 25 years of experience in various fields and markets, he can bring new perspectives to all issues he comes across.

[f] futuristhome
[o] futurist_home
[www] www.futuristhome.com

" *The True Meaning of Holistic Success* "

Nima Hessami

Nima Hessami

Realtor with Norman Hill Realty Inc.

On the fourth day of my most recent ten-day silent retreat, my meditation teacher asked the class to take our routine to the next level. During the previous three days, I had been doing eight sessions of meditation each day, either on my own or as part of a group. Now, my teacher was asking us to try something new: sit down and meditate for an hour WITHOUT moving any part of the body AT ALL! At first, it seemed not a big deal to me, but he warned about the pain we were going to experience and told us, "When you start feeling the numbness and pain in the areas of your body that are touching the ground, just try to observe the pain, bring your attention back to your breath, and let the pain go away." On hearing this, I tried to focus and get prepared for the task in front of me.

You may ask, "A realtor going to a silent retreat for ten days? How did you end up doing that?" In this chapter, I share with you how I became a highly spiritual person, and why I believe this is the cornerstone of whatever success I've achieved in my life.

A Life-Changing Trip

In 2006, I was the president of an annual conference organized by a student organization called AIESEC. AIESEC is an international non-governmental and not-for-profit organisation that provides young people with leadership development, cross-cultural internships, and volunteer exchange experiences. I had just graduated with a double major in engineering and management from McMaster University, and I was planning to apply for internships abroad through my connections at AIESEC.

After my team and I successfully held the annual conference, I applied and received internship offers from various cities around the world, the most exciting of which was Rome, Italy. The position was in an Italian company called Consell Consulting, which provided consulting services to large Italian telecom companies. The internship matched quite well my field of study and my previous internship experience in Toronto, as well as the AIESEC experience, and I was intrigued by the idea of living in Italy of all places! So, I immediately accepted the offer, with my parents' support and encouragement.

My first six months in Italy was an amazing experience.

I was in my mid-twenties, and having the time of my life living in a new country, making international friends, and gaining experience at an Italian company. I made a lot of short weekend trips to different cities in Italy during that period, which broadened my vision of life. Of course, living in a foreign country came with its own hardships too, the main one being the language barrier. You see, although we mainly communicated in English while at work, Italians rarely spoke English outside the work environment. I believe Italians are very proud of their language, and most of them will choose not to speak English even though they may have the proficiency to do so. Therefore, I had a really hard time communicating with the Italian people. Since I was on my own and there was nobody else to turn to, I started teaching myself the language in my spare time, which was not the easiest task in the world, as you can imagine. But I overcame that challenge!

After about six months at Consell, my managers let me know there was an opportunity for me to go to Madrid, Spain to get involved in one of Consell's international projects with the giant Spanish Telecom company, O2. I was over the moon with joy and announced to everyone around me that I was soon relocating to Madrid.

I then came back to Toronto, Canada for the Christmas Holidays. Shockingly, after a few days, I got an email from Consell informing me that the deal with O2 was canceled, and I was not going to Spain after all.

I was badly shaken. Not only was the Spain opportunity gone, but I also felt terrible because I had (prematurely) announced to everyone that I was going to Madrid, and now everyone would think I was full of baloney. I felt pretty bad about this, and this experience taught me a valuable lesson.

I went back to Italy, but this time I had lost my previously established position, and I had to take care of random tasks at work, waiting for a proper project to show up. The first night after I returned, I realized my roommate had brought in a replacement for me. That night I slept on the floor. I felt alone and uncertain of what the future held.

Opening My Eyes Wider

Fortunately, I already had good friends in Italy. One of them picked me up the next day and gave me a ride to another friend's place, who took me in as his new roommate.

This new place was quite a bit farther from work than where I previously lived. Over the next few months, I took a 30-minute bus ride to work every day, which started to open my eyes to a new reality. The bus passed some run-down neighborhoods in Rome which were home to a poorer population. The passengers on the bus reflected this reality very well, as the majority were fairly poor people and refugees from third world countries. I quickly realized not everybody in Rome was living a well-off comfortable life. I started to remove my rose-colored glasses and began to contemplate how most of Roman society lived.

Around that same time, I began to study self-help books, such as the *7 Habits of Highly Successful People* by Stephen Covey, and spiritual books, like the Koran and the Bible. The more I observed the world around me and the more I studied these books, the more aware I became of the fact there are a lot of people around the world who are under-privileged. I began to wonder how I could help bring them peace and comfort.

Back to Canada

After I finished my internship at Consell Consulting, I returned to Canada. But this time I was not completely sure if telecom was the right career for me. While I had enjoyed the management and marketing aspects of my internships, both in Canada and Italy, I wasn't particularly fond of purely engineering jobs, especially ones that involved coding or doing calculations in a room all by myself. I liked to be among others and use my communication skills to build relationships.

I had also developed a keen interest in the workings of the human mind, and through my extensive studies, I started thinking about putting together a training program on this topic and taking it to the corporate world.

A Peek into Real Estate

I continued applying for jobs in traditional engineering companies while thinking about how I could take my productivity training into the corporate world. Nothing significant was coming from the applications, and although I received some job offers, I didn't like those prospects at all. At the same time, a few acquaintances discouraged me from trying the corporate training proposal, saying it was not a good enough idea to go anywhere.

During this period of time, the field of real estate caught my attention as a potential career path. My dad and his partner were already active in the field, building custom-built houses in Toronto. My dad's partner's sons were working with them on the projects too. One day my brother Borna approached me and said, "Nima, why don't we join Dad and his partner and be a part of their team? I'll go and study the building code, and you go and get licensed as a real estate agent. This way, we can all work as a family." Not having another solid alternative, I agreed.

After I signed up for the real estate licensing course, I received a call from a contact at AIESEC who said a friend who did consulting with Bell Canada had a job opening for a tester. Strangely enough, the project involved a real estate web application, and I immediately considered this a sign. I agreed to be a tester, and I started working for the consulting team on an hourly basis while I was completing my real estate courses.

We kept working on the real estate app for a few months until CREA (Canadian Real Estate Association) sued

Bell Canada for disclosing private data, making Bell pull the plug on the project altogether. However, a month later, the same consulting team got another gig from Bell Canada regarding another web application, this time in the extreme sports category. Once again, they asked me to join them as their tester.

This time around, I had my license as a realtor and had joined a commercial real estate brokerage. I was also taking care of my dad's listings and managing his properties for him. However, since I didn't see real estate as my main career path and treated it just as a side hustle to help the family and earn some income, I was still open to opportunities in the engineering field. So, I said yes to the tester job offer.

Getting Serious about Charity

On my bus rides to work, I resumed my study of spiritual and self-help books. In the process, I became more and more mindful that all religions and spiritual teachings had these core teachings in common: Faith and Action. And a part of taking the right action was to help orphans in the community. I liked this concept a lot, because I believed if you help in the proper upbringing of orphans, you're not only helping them build a better life, you're also protecting society from a future social outcast.

I did a lot of research and found there were no orphanages in Toronto. Nonetheless, there were homeless youth shelters. I found one of these shelters at the YMCA and signed up as a volunteer to help youth with their employability.

Neither was I the first nor the only one in my household to do this. Charitable behavior and spirituality have always run in my family. I've been blessed to have a mom, dad and grandparents who have always attached great value to helping others. Maybe, one of the very first people who planted this seed in my mind was my late maternal grandmother, one of the purest souls I've ever met. She was the personification of a kind-hearted serving human being.

Getting More Clarity on the Career Path

I needed to get clarity on what I really wanted to do professionally for the rest of my life. I started to do a lot of self-reflection. In a journal I began writing about my personality, likes and dislikes, skills, background, ambitions and passions. It became more and more clear to me that I didn't like most engineering jobs, such as coding. Instead, I loved anything that involved high-level thinking and was people centered.

However, the idea of abandoning engineering altogether was scary. Was choosing "real estate agent" as a career path the right thing to do? Yes, I had made a commitment to my brother to join the family business, but I doubted if I wanted to become a full-time real estate agent. I kept telling myself, "Anyone can become a realtor. You have done a double major in engineering at one of the best schools in Canada. Do you want to leave that path and become a realtor?"

On the other hand, I thought I could be a unique realtor. I didn't have to be a typical everyday real estate agent. I could be the realtor who had the engineering and management background. There were also other traits that could differentiate me from the pack: my experience of living in Italy, my charitable involvements, my martial arts background, etc.

One day when I was working on the web application project, my boss called me to his office. He said he had received reports that I wasn't fully present at work and that I was often on the phone taking care of my real estate business. He let me know he wasn't happy with my sub-optimal results, and since the project was winding down too, he needed to cut down on my hours at work. I got the message, and I voluntarily quit.

Going All In

I believe everything happens for a reason. Given all my self-reflections, I took this chain of events as a sign that I needed to focus on real estate as my main career path. I had also made a commitment to my brother. In addition, I had started to make a fair bit of money taking care of my dad's listings over the past few months. I eventually made the leap, now fully determined to dedicate myself to real estate and become great at it.

That's why, after interviewing twelve major brokerages in Toronto, I signed with Norman Hill Realty Inc., where I've been a realtor since 2009. There were several good things about this brokerage that attracted me in the first place. First, Norman Hill Realty doesn't just buy and sell residential properties; they are active in commercial real estate too. Second, their office is posh and organized, and they deliver a high-end experience to their clients, which I particularly liked at the time. Third, they work with large builders such as Menkes, Mattamy Homes, etc., which opens a lot of doors for any agent working with them. And finally, the brokerage has a very good sense of belonging.

At my first visit, I met a few respected people who inspired me to sign with Norman Hill. One of them was Helen Norris, a strongly established realtor with more than fifty years of experience, who told me when she first saw me, "Nima, I have a strong intuition. You have something about you that tells me you will be very successful in this field. Just be determined and do whatever it takes." She later became a grandma figure for me, for which I'm eternally grateful.

Slow but Steady

After a couple of years in real estate, I hit six figures, and I've consistently had great income ever since. On the construction side, my brother and I have been working as a team for almost ten years now. I find and buy the land for our client's and our construction projects; he takes care of the actual construction, while I perform the project and budget management, from getting the permit and finding the right architect to hiring subcontractors. And finally, my team and I sell the finished custom homes.

We're very happy that 80% of our business is through referrals and repeat clients, and rarely have we had a dissatisfied customer throughout all these years. We've been fortunate to partner with great investors and other builders along the way, and we're slowly but steadily growing our business to the next level.

I am proud to say our top values are honesty and professionalism, and we are known for delivering exceptional service to our clients. At this moment, I have thirty-seven five-star reviews on my Google rating, which tells the reader a lot about who I am and what I do.

I very much enjoy my career as a realtor, and I particularly like that it gives me the freedom to pay attention and fulfill other important areas of my life. I have big dreams about the future, and what makes me different from most other realtors is my unique definition of holistic success.

My Chair Model of Success

I have been a volunteer at the Horizons for Youth Shelter

in Toronto for almost seven years now. This is a shelter that caters to about forty young homeless men and women between the ages of 16 and 26, a large percentage of whom are refugees. Also among them are youngsters recovering from addiction and others with mental health issues not serious enough to need major medical treatment. I started off as a volunteer teaching youth about employability. Later I switched to a coaching position, where I teach them a course in life skills using my Chair Model of Success.

In that course, I share with them what I've experienced true success to be. This is a model which I perfected over the years, setting its foundation when I came back from Italy in 2007, and to this day I practice it. I strongly believe success is not all about earning more money or becoming financially well-off. Of course, money is important, but I believe what is more important is to have a holistic approach to a balanced life. I tell the youth that a successfully balanced lifestyle is very much like a chair. Any comfortable chair has four legs and a comfortable cushion, and it's strongly rooted on the ground. Success is very much like that.

The first chair leg is **financial stability**, which is all about having enough income to be self-sufficient and be able to support yourself and those who are dependent on you. In order to get there, you need to choose the right career. If you want to succeed professionally, begin with the end in mind. Decide where you want to be twenty to thirty years from now (or longer), and then work your way back to the present moment. You will then have clarity on exactly what you should do now to get closer to your ultimate goal. This approach of beginning with the end in mind is applicable in all aspects of life and other parts of the Chair Model of Success as well.

The second leg of the chair is **physical health**, which is all about making sure you get the right nutrition, regular exercise, and enough sleep. I believe in order to be successful professionally, you need to take care of your temple (i.e. body). I have been mindful of my health all my life. I'm quite advanced in my swimming skills: I'm a certified lifeguard, and I was even the pool assistant manager as a teenager. I've also attained a second Dan in Taekwondo, and I've been a coach to new Taekwondo students and a referee in some competitions. I believe the discipline and sense of responsibility one learns as a Taekwondo practitioner are priceless. Having any proper exercise routine is key in leading a healthy lifestyle.

The third leg is your **mental health/education**. How do you make sure that you can enter the right career that will lead you to financial freedom? You guessed correctly: through education and training. That's why I over-emphasize to the youth at the shelter the importance of finishing their studies. Over these years, I've been fortunate enough to see quite a few of these youth finish high school, and even college, and go on to build a bright future for themselves.

There's a correlation between physical and mental health too. Taking the same care to keep physically healthy— proper exercise, diet, and sleep—contributes to mental health. Meditation also plays a very important role.

The fourth leg of the Chair Model of Success is **relationships**, which includes your intimate and social relationships. I always tell the youth at the shelter, "You may have come from a dysfunctional family, but remember, you can always choose your friends. You might not have been in control about choosing your parents, but you definitely can choose the people who surround you. And ultimately you can choose the family you plan on creating. Forming wholesome relationships over the years on the basis of pure love and trust, and resolving any bad ones, will prove very valuable in your life.

We now have the four legs in place, but in order for the chair to be in balance, the length of the legs must be equal. In other words, if we just focus on your work life and neglect your health or relationships, you will not be truly successful. Similarly, if you spend a lot of time on your social relationships but are not strategic about your professional growth, you will not reach the level of success that you have always wanted.

How about the cushion? What is it that actually makes the chair more comfortable to use, and how does it relate to your life of wanting comfort? When I ask the youths this question, they inevitably answer, after a short pause: **"Fun and enjoyment**." That's why it's so important to take the time to develop hobbies and have fun with friends and family on a regular basis.

Okay, we have a chair with four legs and a comfy cushion. But is that all? What keeps the chair rooted to the ground and keeps it from floating away? You're right. Gravity. Interestingly, you can't see gravity, but it's still there to give the chair stability.

When you think of success, that gravitational force is your **spiritual health**, which is all about having a good intention in everything you do. That's the key invisible force that guarantees your success long term: making sure you are in the right mind-set, thought-set and heart-set in all areas of your life, from dealing with your customers to your family relationships.

I always tell the youth at the shelter to go out in nature and observe the amazing pure energy and infinite intelligence that is guiding the whole universe in an immaculate fashion. I believe just being more conscious of this energy keeps you connected to the source and leads to a more fulfilled life. You will then be in tune with this positive guiding energy which ensures you are on the right path.

Another key part of spiritual health is serving other people, especially those who do not have your good fortune. Sometimes, it's about helping them financially, or giving of your intellect and skills, and sometimes it's about spending time with them so they can experience periods of happiness amid their tough circumstances.

That's why, in addition to volunteering at the youth shelter, I also volunteer at the school division of the Holland Bloorview Kids Rehabilitation Hospital in Toronto one morning each week. There I am an assistant gym teacher, contributing to the well-being of the children who are going through treatment at the hospital and helping to brighten their days.

As for this Chair Model of Success, what is the by-product of all its facets? Happiness, peace and harmony. The results of a holistic approach to a balanced life, where all important aspects of your life—financial stability, physical health, mental health/education, relationships, fun/hobbies and spiritual health—are all being nourished. Doing so will ensure you're taking the right steps to make you and those around you successful, and ultimately feeling happy and fulfilled.

The interesting thing about the Chair Model of Success is that all of us tend to go off balance quite often. Usually the main culprit is too much focus on work. I strive to take notice whenever I'm going off balance and take action to restore that equilibrium.

I believe I have described the ultimate meaning of success, and I truly hope everyone can become more conscious of this Chair Model of Success and truly apply it in their own lives to reap the sweet benefits.

The True Meaning of Holistic Success

Author's Bio

Nima Hessami's involvement in Toronto's Real Estate industry since 2004 has gained him the Commercial and Residential Broker status as well as the SRS (Seller's Representative Specialist) and RENE (Real Estate Negotiation Expert) designations. Nima's areas of expertise are in Infill Land Assembly/Development and Custom Luxury Home Building and Sales, with secondary focus in Investment Properties in Mid Toronto, North York, Thornhill and Richmond Hill.

Nima is part of a dedicated Real Estate and Construction team with over 50 years of experience who focus on Land Assembly and Building "Smart" Luxury Homes by engaging the investor community in Land Syndication and Joint Venture projects.

Nima's Real Estate arm operates out of Norman Hill Realty's office in Markham, Ontario and the Construction arm operates under Panrock Developments Inc., in Toronto, Ontario as Panrock Homes.

On a personal level, Nima is a long time community and sports enthusiast with a 2nd Dan degree in Taekwondo and engagements for various community bounding initiatives benefiting a Homeless Youth Shelter and Sick Kid's Rehab Hospital.

You can learn more about Nima's business and personal activities via the following channels:

- www.hessme.com
- www.panrockhomes.com
- www.facebook.com/HessMe.Realty
- www.instagram.com/hessme.realty
- www.instagram.com/panrockhomes

"Delivering Luxury and Work Ethic"

Maryam Jalilalghadr

Maryam Jalilalghadr

Real Estate Agent

It's sometimes unfathomable how you may end up enjoying a job that, at some point in the past, you thought you'd never do! I'm an engineer turned real estate agent who specializes in luxury properties in the Forest Hill area of Toronto. I'm going to share with you the interesting story of how I entered real estate and what has been the driving force for my success in one of the hottest industries in North America.

Engineer by Training

Although my father is a successful businessman, and my family has long been surrounded by top-tier businesspeople, education holds high value in my family. I always ranked among the top students in high school, and my parents—especially my dad—placed a huge emphasis on studying well.

After immigrating to Canada, I complemented my academic orientation as an electrical engineer and master's student in International Law by completing two career advancement courses. I spent a few years learning material in power engineering and electronic and computer engineering at BCIT (British Columbia Institute of Technology) in Vancouver.

After graduation, I started looking for a job. Around the same time, a recession hit North America, so jobs were scarce. However, in my search, I came across several positions suited to my area of expertise. I decided to apply for one that seemed more academically oriented, while I passed on some other opportunities involving companies merely interested in business. I applied for and landed a position as a lab technician at the NRC, National Research Council, a government institution bubbling with bright scientists within an academic environment. At NRC, I joined a team which adapted fuel cells already being used in spaceships in order to be used in automobiles.

Simultaneously, I sat for six gruelling board exams and studied hard for my registered engineer designation with the APEGBC, the Association of Professional Engineers and Geoscientists in British Columbia. This was a daunting task for me. Not only was I trying to settle down in a completely new country, but I also just had a new baby and had to take care of two children, 12-year-old Deniz and baby Doreen. As always, I felt the heartwarming support of my husband Morteza, who was completing his PhD in oncology at UBC, University of British Columbia, and working at the BC Cancer Research Center.

After many months of exams, I succeeded in obtaining my registered engineer designation and was honored with the engineering ring. This ring, a meaningful symbol, serves as a reminder to each engineer who receives one to live by a high standard of professional conduct.

Sanctions, Recession, and More

Morteza and I had few financial worries in those days, as we had brought in plenty of funds to meet our needs as new immigrants in Canada. However, in 2011, everything changed. New sanctions against Iran had been passed, the value of the rial against the dollar fell at an unbelievable rate, and our back-up properties, purchased before immigration, lost their values. This served as a shocking revelation and eye-opener for Morteza and me. Meanwhile, the Canadian economy suffered from a harsh recession, so the prospect of Morteza securing a good position after completing his PhD seemed slim.

For the first time in our lives, we felt financially insecure. We faced the cold hard truth: We couldn't support ourselves financially for much longer if we didn't get more serious about making money in Canada.

Whaaat? Real Estate?

When we first came to Canada, everybody, including my husband, told me, "You must get into real estate." They considered me sociable, in addition to believing in my attention to detail and top-notch taste. I laughed at the proposition in the beginning. I responded, "Real estate? You must be kidding. I'm an academic person, an engineer. What has real estate got to do with someone like me?" At this point, it's hard to believe I'm the same person who once said that.

Morteza and I rented a house for our first few years in Vancouver, but in 2007, we decided to buy our first property. I was in no rush, so I took my time and spent a whole year searching. All weekend long, I would attend open houses. I think I went to 500 of them in total! It was simply fun to do, not to mention the fact that I enjoyed the experience because of my love for interior design and architecture. I also used my analytical engineering mind to run numbers in my head and compare data from the houses I visited. Eventually, I found my ideal property, negotiated the deal with the seller myself, and hired an agent to make the offer for me. It was such a great experience and left me feeling exhilarated throughout. I began to realize that real estate is something I'm passionate about.

Moving to Toronto

Morteza accepted a post-doc position offered by the University of Toronto, so we decided to move to the city of opportunities. Good positions remained rare in Vancouver, and we felt motivated to eliminate the insecurity of depending on our monetary assets from Iran. Although moving to a new city was no small undertaking, it elicited such a great response from our friends in Vancouver. They exclaimed, "Wow! You're living a stable life here. You don't *have* to move to Toronto for this opportunity, but look at you, challenging yourselves. You're taking a risk and going for something better. Good for you!" We were energized.

Again, I put myself to work. I rented our house in Vancouver, found a property manager to take care of the house while we were away, found and rented a great property in Toronto.

We initially intended to stay in Toronto for two years, until Morteza finished his post-doc, and then return to Vancouver. However, we recognized that more opportunities for Morteza would exist in Toronto in the long run, and despite my sheer love of Vancouver, we elected to stay. I took the lead with the real estate part of our resettling process. I found a great home for us in Toronto, negotiated the deal, bought it with the help of an agent, and subsequently sold our Vancouver house. I kept acquiring more experience in real estate, and strangely enough, I was loving it.

Now that Morteza and I had decided to stay in Toronto and Doreen was not a baby anymore, I needed to choose what to do professionally. I had two realistic options on the table. First, I could fully commit to my field of study and pursue a career in engineering. Second, I could dedicate myself to real estate, this newfound passion of mine. I explored the first option for a short while, even found positions that fit my skills, but I eventually decided against it. I came up with several reasons to support my decision. The jobs I found required long commutes through the busy streets of Toronto, which I didn't like.

Also, I wanted to be close to my children and spend more time with them at home. Furthermore, as a bit of a perfectionist, I believed I didn't have enough solid experience working as an engineer. Instead, I wanted to go into a field I both loved and felt more confident about. The obvious choice was real estate.

The decision to pursue real estate full-time felt just right to me. I have always advocated for equal pay and equal opportunities for men and women. I felt bothered seeing women earning far less money than men in the exact same positions. The field of real estate provided equal opportunity to play and earn for both men and women, and naturally this appealed to me. Engineers typically experience some discrimination based on the school they attended or based on gender. In real estate, though, everyone becomes licensed through the same organization—RECO, the Real Estate Council of Ontario—and equal commissions are made by men and women. This prospect deeply excited me.

I felt confident enough to dedicate myself fully to real estate due to the experience I gained by going to hundreds of showings and by buying, selling, and renting our family properties. I had negotiated very large transactions over the previous few years and now had no fear of sorting out any deal. I had seen it all; well, not all, but most of it! Since all of the properties I sold and bought for our family turned out to be of good value, I felt confident in my ability to make great choices in real estate.

On top of all these reasons, I possessed a very strong work ethic, a key asset for anyone in the real estate industry. I knew that not every realtor's personality shared my attention to detail, powerful sense of responsibility, and belief in giving exclusively high-quality service. To my delight, Morteza backed my decision, too.

Going All In

I devoted the next 18 months of my life to taking the necessary courses and six required RECO exams in order to obtain my real estate license. Given my commitment to my family, going through this process truly tested me. After overcoming a few bumps along the road, I finally managed to graduate successfully from the courses and pass all exams.

The next step for me involved choosing my brokerage. More than a few very big brokerage firms exist in the Toronto real estate environment, including ReMax,

RoyalLePage, HomeLife, Forest Hill, Harvey Kalles, and Keller Williams. I planned to interview with some of them to find the best option.

To determine which one could be the best fit for me, I established specific criteria. I didn't care for the mass-produced and industrial feel of some brokerages, where the focus is mainly on the number of transactions. Instead, I preferred a smaller brokerage that presented itself as more exclusive and boutique-style, providing exemplary customer service and focusing on long-term client relationships. Ultimately, two options stood out for me: Forest Hill and Harvey Kalles.

After a lot of soul searching and market research, I finally decided to join Forest Hill Brokerage. Several factors motivated that decision. First, the central office of Forest Hill is very close to my home, so I'd be farming where I live, so to speak. Second, Forest Hill's clients and style of care resembled exactly what I pictured for my ideal brokerage: exclusive, high-end, and sophisticated. Third, I used their services when buying our home in Forest Hill a few years back. I felt familiar with their style of doing business, and I liked it. Last, but not least, I saw a great opportunity to create awareness within the Persian community about this posh area of Toronto. Most families in this demographic had not seriously considered this great neighborhood as an option to live or invest in.

Meanwhile, Morteza secured a position as a faculty member at U of T, an amazing career step. It seemed worth it to have left our comfortable life in Vancouver and taken such a big risk moving to Toronto. Everything would turn out surprisingly great... or would it?

Complications

Any new business comes with challenges, and mine was no exception. After joining Forest Hill, the primary challenge seemed clear: How do I find clients?

I made a rather wise decision to join a team of experienced realtors in the same office with a record of success. This team consisted of an experienced couple who had worked in the industry for more than twenty years and had become well-known and established in the neighborhood.

This decision may be among the best I ever made in my real estate career. I built success within my unique position alongside that couple, because I held no expectation they would share their commissions with me, a novice real estate agent. In the same way these two built a reputation over twenty years, I knew the only person who could develop my progress in real estate was me. Only I could create the kind of results I wanted.

Remarkably, I began getting the results I wanted. I benefited from huge visibility, because my partners included me on their widely distributed ads. I received numerous calls from those ads, which turned into great leads for my business. Once, the deputy minister of education in BC contacted me after seeing one of the advertisements.

Our team's open houses allowed me to connect with solid prospects who eventually turned into clients, sometimes for multiple future properties. A feat I strived to one day accomplish involved an unrepresented client hiring me during an open house to make an offer on the property, on the spot.

At the start of my career, I implemented a strategy based on reliability and presence. When attending open houses, I placed my signs beside the street every single weekend. I posted on my Facebook and Instagram accounts about the listings. My circle of contacts could see that I was an active agent in the market. The neighborhood soon grew familiar with my name, too. Yes, the signs cost me money to print, and the open houses took time away from my family on weekends.

I experienced some long stretches of time when no business came in despite all the time, money, and energy invested in open houses. However, overall I kept getting more visibility, learned like crazy, and continued getting new leads while making connections in social settings. What more could I have asked for?

Coming to a Halt

After working with the realtor couple for a while, I experienced something rare. I was finishing up at an open house around 4:00 pm on a Saturday, when I heard someone knocking at the front door. I opened the door to find a lady apologizing for being late and asking to come in and see the house. Although the showing time was officially over, I let her in. It turned out that she worked as a physician and had come directly from a seminar in downtown Toronto, hoping to catch the open house in the nick of time. I showed the house to her, and she loved it. She asked me to represent her in making an offer on the house.

My determination finally proved worthwhile: an unrepresented buyer requested me to purchase the house for her in the same moment I was showing it via open house. I thought, "Yes! The hard work has eventually paid off."

I prepared the offer for my new client and presented it to the listing agent later that day. Since our offer price landed way below the asking price, the listing agent warned me, "This is very low. I don't think we can do this. Let me handle it. I'll let you know. Thanks."

The following day, I received a call from the listing agent, informing me that she had received another better offer, and naturally the seller accepted that one, instead.

I was so disappointed with this outcome and felt down for days on end. I thought, "This is pointless. I'm getting nothing in return for all the energy I'm putting in. I'm dedicating all my weekends to open houses, and I haven't been able to secure even one single client. Perhaps the naysayers are right, and I'm too naive to be working under this arrangement." I felt tempted to leave the team.

I'm happy I didn't decide to do so in a rush, because when my strong emotions subsided, I realized that minor failure is simply part of the game. The real estate industry involves tight competition. From a business perspective, the listing agents did nothing wrong; they merely protected their own interests.

I knew that if I wanted to make it big in real estate, I needed to continue improving my skills. I could learn to manage situations like that better in the future, and I needed to take responsibility. I possessed control of the creation of my reality and should not blame other people for the challenges I faced. I didn't want to behave like some professionals who change their team or brokerage each time they run into a problem. I believed running away wouldn't help. Rather, I needed to improve myself.

I chose to stay on the team, and I grew a lot from that experience. To this day, I maintain a respectful relationship with the couple.

What Sets Me Apart in Real Estate

Several of my personality traits set me apart from most realtors in the market. First, I'm overly patient. In one case, I prepared around 20 offers for a group of builders before they finally purchased land for their construction project. I understand that buying and selling real estate takes time. For buyers, the process involves one of the biggest financial investments in life and still involves a lot of money for those selling. I never rush my clients to make decisions. Other agents might stop investing time in a client if they attend three or four showings and the client has not made up their mind yet. I'm exactly the opposite. I may spend a year or two with a client before they finally give the green light.

Furthermore, I pay exemplary attention to detail. When I coordinate an open house, I take care of every single detail, and I deliver an immaculate presentation. People love my showings and really seem to see the difference. Attendees notice how I go the extra mile when I'm at the open house, and they appreciate it.

In addition, I'm all for educating the client. I believe clients must have a decent amount of information to make a calculated decision. The responsibility of educating the client falls on their agent. For this reason, I take the time and energy to give my clients all the information they need so they will be thrilled with the end result of our searching.

Finding the Right Agent

Reader, if you're not an agent yourself, you may need to hire one to sell or buy your property. I believe the right agent for you is one who:

- doesn't judge you when you ask them questions.

- you're comfortable with sharing your concerns.

- is patient enough to educate you until reaching the point when you're ready to make the right decision.

Future Plans

Right now, I'm totally focused on growing my network and my business. Down the road, I have plans for starting my own brokerage. I consider moving back to Vancouver in a few years, and if I do, I might open the first Forest Hill brokerage there, which is really exciting.

Tips for New Real Estate Agents

I would love to leave new agents with these three tips:

- Success takes time. A new business is like a baby. You need to nourish it, nurture it, and look after it. There's no pressure cooker for your business that will help you skip steps. Consistency over time pays off. If you're in need of immediate income, I warn you that real estate is a long-term game. If you're desperate about making money, you won't be able to provide great service and will likely be stressed out most of the time. If you're married and a new realtor, I suggest that your partner secure a fixed income while you venture into real estate as a long-term strategy.

- Take responsibility. It is up to *you* to create your own results. No one owes you anything, and nobody will care about your success as much as you do. Take charge, put in the work, and enjoy the process.

- Work ethic is everything. I strongly believe this, maybe because it runs in my family. My Dad often told us, "Good name is all you've got. Reputation isn't something you can buy or sell. You have to earn it and protect it. It's very delicate. If it's broken, there's no way of fixing it."

Delivering Luxury and Work Ethic

Author's Bio

Maryam Jalilalghadr offers an

immaculate real estate service backed by her strong work ethic and determination. She'll never rush anybody to make an uninformed decision. She'll take the time to educate her clients, and she'll answer all their questions. She is there until they are completely ready to decide.

She is the realtor with strong work ethic who specializes in luxury properties in mid-town Toronto.

Forest Hill is her neighborhood, where she has raised her two daughters. She is very knowledgeable and passionate about this beautiful area.

"35 Years in Commercial Real Estate"

Stephen Katz

Stephen Katz

Head of Commercial Real Estate at HLC

I have always loved science. Throughout most of my time in school, I considered myself a very good student who excelled with numbers. After grade 11, I was admitted into a program for advanced students called MISP (Modular Integrated Science Program). I'm originally from Montreal, but I left Quebec after one year in this MISP program and moved to London, Ontario, to study biology at The University of Western Ontario.

I skipped year 1 and started university in year 2 of an Honours Biology BSc program. My goal was to get into medical school, but my grades would not support that desire. I was earning Cs instead of As and having a good time making new friends and going to parties. Instead of choosing the smarter and more patient path, to take more courses and improve my grades, I decided to finish quickly by completing courses that would get me a 3-year BSc degree.

I remember clearly the moment I decided to get into real estate. While taking a plant sciences course, we worked on a project that required collecting samples from different types of trees. I found myself up in a tree collecting leaf samples, and I suddenly asked myself, "What am I doing up here? What am I really going to do with my life?"

At that point, I knew my grades wouldn't qualify me for admission to medical school, so becoming a doctor was off the table. Also, I didn't want to end up working with my dad, who owned his own women's sportswear manufacturing business. Although his was a successful business, my dad believed it was a "sunset industry" and did not foresee a long-term future for that endeavor.

My dad always did his best to help when I asked for it, so I approached him with my question of what to do for my career. First, he set up a business lunch for me with a lawyer, a doctor, and an accountant. Interestingly enough, each one had a disgruntlement issue with his job. Next, my father asked one of his closest friends, Seymore Obront, to take me under his wing. Seymore was a leader in the shopping center industry, and he hired me to work at Snowcap Investments. At nineteen years of age, I must have been the youngest ever shopping center consultant.

Snowcap consulted for fifty-two national retail clients for which they identified and negotiated new store locations in enclosed shopping centers across Canada.

Working with Mr. Obront, I learned a lot about real estate, especially within the shopping mall industry. During my four years of employment, I grew familiar with leases and all the clauses and details that go in them. I realized that contrary to common belief, leases are the cornerstone of real estate, rather than buying and selling. I also understood that every property is worth the underlying value of its lease[1]. In other words, if you understand the lease, you can understand the value of a commercial property. This concept functions in stark contrast to how things work in residential real estate.

After leaving Snowcap, the real estate department at WHSmith Books hired me. I appreciated the job, but my primary task of reviewing leases all day became tedious, and I believed I needed to improve my business skills. I quit after only a few months, because the repetitive nature of the position was driving me crazy. I wanted to

---

1 A helpful equation in determining the value of a property: NOI (net operating income) / Cap. rate (capitalization rate) = Value. For more information about this, reach out to me.

build my business skillset and ultimately land a higher paying job. For these reasons, I decided to go back to school and earn an MBA.

Back to School

I wrote my GMATs and began researching MBA schools. The United States housed many more schools with what I perceived at the time to offer better quality programs. I also believed that the US economy was stronger and that more job opportunities existed in the States. My family lived in Montreal, so I decided to focus my school search on the Northeastern US. A good number of schools that I applied to offered me acceptance, and I set up interviews. My research preferences, along with my love for skiing, the ocean, and sports all attracted me to Boston College. The first time I visited its campus, I knew it was the right place for me. The people, the campus, and the prestige of the MBA program made the decision easy.

My graduation two years later in 1991 coincided with what I like to call the global real estate lead recession. This recession affected the Canadian market as much as anywhere else. Federated Allied stores filed for bankruptcy protection, and many overvalued real estate properties were unable to service their debt. Many real estate developers and shopping center companies stopped hiring, and the job search became challenging. I wanted to stay in Boston and considered working as a real estate agent with a large brokerage based there. Initially, my efforts to get hired did not go well. I believe my challenges stemmed partly from being Canadian and partly from not looking like a typical real estate agent. In one memorable interview, I was told, "You're not what we typically look for when hiring a real estate agent."

For the first time, I responded by telling the brokerage firm the real estate industry was changing and clients would more likely value someone with good analytical skills than someone who looked like a car salesman. Real estate business is not as straightforward as the selling of most other products, perhaps because property is the single largest entity someone can sell. In both size and monetary value, real estate surpasses designer clothes, cars, and even airplanes. Therefore, the skillset necessary for achieving desired results in this industry must be different. I quickly came to understand that if I wanted to succeed in real estate, I should focus on the current trends, the types of people who actually own real estate, and the primary needs of employers.

I soon realized my MBA degree was not going to guarantee getting hired and that relying on my previous work experience and contacts would better help me to secure a job. I reconsidered basing myself in Canada as an option.

My economic knowledge informed me that in times of recessions, real estate goes back to the banks. For this reason, I reached out to my contacts in Canada to help connect me with opportunities in banks. I was then introduced to the Senior Vice President of a newly formed Real Estate Department at Scotiabank. I ended up working with this gentleman for the next twenty-five years.

RED

The Real Estate Department (RED) at Scotiabank was first established with a team of four people each bringing their own special skills to the table. The vice president was a great strategist with extensive real estate skills. The director possessed strong business skills and already worked in another department at the bank, and me, a young, analytical-minded real estate professional who enjoyed working with spreadsheets and quantifying everything.

I was originally hired as an Asset Manager and quickly found my niche working on retail, industrial, hotel, shopping malls, office and all types of real estate situations The four of us collaborated on projects which included preparing carefully crafted memos for executives on various real estate matters. All four of us would edit the memo and it would not go through to the executive until we were certain the document included sound ideas, correct numbers, and well-thought-out recommendations. Our team began working on a few development projects and earned recognition for our strengths and capabilities.

I was soon promoted to Senior Asset Manager within months after being hired. My colleagues and I continued receiving praise for our real estate and decision-making skills, and our department grew very quickly. Our group took charge of leasing, construction, property management, architects, accounting, and legal advice. Our team also grew from four people to one hundred fifty in a relatively short time.

I used my strong analytical skills to move projects forward and worked on multiple large projects in all the realty functions and in many different markets.

My international experience expanded even further, as Scotiabank purchased Banco Inverlat in Mexico and continued its international focus to become the most wide-reaching of all the Canadian Banks. During my tenure at Scotiabank, I was fortunate to negotiate leases and work on purchases and sales across Canada, in ten major US cities, Puerto Rico, Jamaica, Mexico, London, and Cairo.

My Analytical Skills at Work

Around 1996, Scotiabank's CEO wanted to know whether the bank would be better off buying or leasing its properties. I ran a comprehensive analytical study on the entire portfolio of Scotiabank's real estate holdings. I then worked with stakeholders to determine the key variables for wanting to own a location, rather than leasing it. Ranking each variable, such as branch profitability, I identified which properties seemed the best candidates to own.

Next, I drafted a memo explaining that if the bank wanted to reduce its exposure to real estate risk, the ratio of owned-to-leased properties should be 1:1. I based this proposition on the fact that real estate is cyclical in nature. A landlord's market exists when vacancy rates are low, available space is leased quickly, and rental rates are high. A tenant's market, by contrast, exists when vacancy rates are high, space stays on the market for some time, tenant inducements and free rents increase, and net effective rents drop.

Scotiabank executives naturally recognized that the entity's expertise lay in the banking business, not in real estate. To reduce the bank's exposure to fluctuations in the real estate cycle, the executive department agreed with my memo and approved our efforts to buy real estate in order to bring the ownership-to-lease ratio from about 33% to 50%.

Interestingly, a few years later, the other major Canadian banks all began to sell much of their real estate. The reported reasons for these actions were that the return on equity (ROE) they could receive from their banking business was around 15%, and real estate provided returns of around 8%. My analytical skills came into play, and we communicated to our executives the benefits of owning real estate, despite the trend we had observed. I believed that each property should be compared against other investments in its same asset class. One cannot simply compare the return from real estate to the return on equity from the bank. Just because the bank makes a 15% ROE, that does not mean every investment must return 15%. For example, let's say a bond has a return of 3%, which is acceptable as an asset class. However, this does not mean that one should not buy real estate at 8%. Each form of investment needs to be considered on its own. However, if real estate is trading at 8%, and someone will buy property at 6%, then it is clearly a good idea to sell.

In the end, our department's communications were well received and approved by executives, so we began to buy properties while other banks continued to sell. Our strategy ultimately proved successful, once rental rates started increasing and our exposure to these increases noticeably diminished. The largest acquisition accomplished by our department was that of Scotia Plaza. I worked with the RED team to purchase this two-million-square-foot office property. My roles included conducting the valuation of the property, creating a spreadsheet to understand the cost of the distressed preferred shares, and drafting the all-important memo to executives to obtain the required approvals. I was around 30 years old at the time and felt very proud of my contribution to this historical purchase.

I recall another instance when my analytical skills enabled me to help Scotiabank executives make the right decisions, while going against the prevalent wisdom. At one time, all the other banks were raising their tier-one capital ratios, meaning they were electing to increase the amount of cash on hand. These banks primarily utilized sale-leasebacks to accomplish this status. In a sale-leaseback, an owner of a property sells the property and immediately leases the space in order to become the tenant of the new owner. I recall that I was asked to look at a recent string of sale-leasebacks by Spain's Bank Santander and determine if these transactions would make sense for Scotiabank to employ.

I weighed the pros and cons to this strategy and, as always, prepared a spreadsheet to quantify the benefit of owning versus leasing. I arrived at the strong opinion this technique did not make sense for the major Canadian banks. A sale-leaseback realistically involved the seller borrowing money from the buyer and later paying them back at a set interest rate. I argued, "Banks lend money to others, and therefore should not be borrowing money through sale-leasebacks. If a bank positions itself as a borrower, then it effectively admits to great weakness and will likely fail."

I seldom minced words, and my bosses did not prefer this quality of mine at times. However, in this case, like many others, my analytical approach, quantitative analysis of all alternatives, and clear, well-written memo provided the recipe for success of the Real Estate Department.

My analytical skills were consistently in high demand within the department. I worked on branch acquisitions, most complicated branch leases, many tenant lease situations, landlord leasing, asset management of owned properties, and providing real estate valuation for mergers and acquisitions of other companies by the bank. I thoroughly enjoyed challenges and constantly looked for big projects to become involved in. I contributed to each of the largest projects in the department, including Western Gas Tower and Scotia Centre in Calgary, Tour Scotia in Montreal, One Liberty Plaza in New York City, and 33 Finnsbury Square in London, UK.

In yet another situation, my analytical skills and ability to recognize the value of real estate property assisted the bank in making millions of dollars with no risk. One year, the bank received a 'shotgun' just before Christmas. This term refers to a situation in which a partner exercises a clause forcing other partners to either sell their stake or buy from the offering partner.

The stakes were very high, the real estate market sat at the bottom of its cycle, and the rest of my department wanted to sell. Relying on the cyclical nature of the market, I prepared my Argus software model to acquire an accurate valuation of the property. I verified my assumption, met with senior managers in the department, and started the process to buy the property at the shotgun price. Concurrently, we investigated the potential to re-sell the property. Our legal team timed the transactions so the purchase and the sale occurred within twenty-four hours of each other, resulting in a huge profit in one day, with NO RISK!

Final Projects at Scotiabank

In 2013, the attitude of the bank regarding real estate began to change. The new CEO directed Scotiabank's primary focus toward technology. Our real estate department always existed as a back-office function, and owning real estate was no longer an important concern for the bank. We started to look into the potential sale of bank-owned real estate.

Our department grew extremely busy working with Scotia Capital and Commercial Real Estate Service CBRE on the sale of Scotia Plaza. The $1.27B sale price represented the largest single asset sale in Canada at that time. My role entailed providing my institutional knowledge of the property and assisting with the underwriting. Following this sale, most senior employees in the Real Estate Department began to leave, and I concluded my own twenty-five-year career at Scotiabank in 2015.

I continued to focus my energy on adding value to complicated real estate projects right up until the end of my tenure at the bank. I knew I would be let go before the end of the year in 2015 and willingly stayed on for another handful of months to complete the sale of Scotia Center Saskatoon. This particularly interesting deal involved securing a long-term lease with a lead tenant, then acquiring the leased land so the bank could sell a freehold interest. I recommended and retained Colliers, a commercial real estate company, to sell the property. My asset management skills resulted in adding roughly $6 million in value.

Once I left Scotiabank, I decided to stay away from banks and started calling real estate developers to see if I could find a job with them. I knocked on many doors and sat down with various CEOs I had previously worked with during my time at the bank. However, I struggled to receive offers, since analysts generally were hired into entry level positions, and I did not fit the qualifications for roles of a director or vice president.

After some unfruitful searching, I turned my focus toward large brokerage houses. Many banks outsourced their real estate business, and I believed my combined knowledge of real estate and banking would serve as a significant asset. These next meetings and interviews went much better, and I finally received interest and offers from the brokerage community. However, I did not yet possess a real estate license. Once I gained employment at Colliers, I initiated the process to obtain my real estate license. Working with the Capital Markets team, my first project involved bringing in more business from none other than Scotiabank. Our success resulted in Colliers selling thirteen Scotiabank properties across the country.

Later that year, I earned my real estate license and received an interesting call from Colliers' CEO. He asked if I wanted to work on a newly created program called the Acceleration Program. He designed this initiative to train new agents in ways that would expedite their learning curve in the industry, so they could hit the ground running in only one year. This program acted as a star-hunting endeavor, where I (the numbers guy) coached and trained new recruits alongside two other experts (a strategy guy and a cold-call coach). The three of us developed course content and delivered the entire program at Colliers. I considered us a great team, and in verification of this belief, our course won an award, and many participants provided us with excellent feedback.

After three years at Colliers, one day I heard the company had hired an outside consultant to help standardize procedures and make everything more measurable. A few new faces appeared in the program's administration, and shortly thereafter, both the strategy coach and the technical skills coach (that was my job) were out of work.

Final Push

I found myself out of work once again, but this time, I returned to my plan A, earning money as a real estate agent. I now held a real estate license, so I secured a few listings and lined up several meetings with members of the brokerage community. I met Andrew Cimerman, CEO of HomeLife Realty Services, and decided to join his "higher standards" 5-star team, a perfect opportunity for me. He wanted to create a commercial division and looked to hire an experienced commercial real estate professional who would be willing to recruit and train agents. I joined up right away and started to build my real estate listings and the new commercial team. We decided to brand the commercial division as HLC. Cimerman envisioned his company being known as a 5-Star brand. When people hire a HomeLife realtor, they should be confident they are getting a well-trained agent who will act with honesty and integrity.

I now feel everything has fallen into place for me. I am essentially my own boss. Furthermore, I continually use my strong commercial real estate experience to do real industry-leading work. Unlike my time spent at Scotiabank, I utilize my analytical skills to help the smaller guy in commercial real estate to make the right decision. Our HLC team focuses on asset services, helping landlords retain tenants and lease space; tenant services, helping tenants identify their real estate alternatives and save money through effective and professional negotiations; and investor services, helping clients buy and sell real estate and entire businesses.

A lot of my work with clients begins with their lease agreement, the cornerstone of commercial real estate. Real estate business relies heavily on work relationships, and I believe my skills to be best in class. At this point in my career, I am pleased to work with smaller tenants who reap the benefits of my thirty-five years of experience. If these same clients sought help from larger brokerage houses such as CBRE and Colliers, they would most likely be assigned a newer agent with little or no real experience. I thoroughly enjoy the opportunity to use my skills to save my clients money.

I strongly believe if I continue to do good work, I will steadily acquire more referrals in the future. I have joined a networking group called Business Networking International (BNI), whose motto is "Givers gain." I endeavor to give and provide the absolute most that my skills and experience will allow, and I believe this in turn will allow HLC to become the best new commercial real estate division of any residential brokerages in existence. Perhaps one day, our team might even outperform the largest brokerages. For now, I'm extremely happy to be able to make a difference in the lives of small business owners.

I have a very big vision for the future. What I'm doing at HLC lays the foundation for providing a full range of commercial real estate services to Canadian business owners. I have conducted real estate transactions around the globe and truly value these international experiences. My technical skills are transferable and equally effective all over the world, so I hope I can one day build a team and offer similar services worldwide.

The industry includes countless residential realtors, but very few possess commercial real estate experience as well. This comes as no surprise, because the OREA training program offers very little information regarding commercial real estate and absolutely none on commercial leases. Commercial real estate transactions take on average six to nine months to complete, and since commercial work involves different skills than residential, very specialized training is required. I am providing exactly that at HLC.

Final Words

Two things helped me the most in achieving success in real estate. First, I acquired multi-market knowledge, meaning I am not merely another neighborhood realtor. I worked in numerous cities and markets on a very wide range of projects, including office, retail, industrial, multi-residential, hotel, and development.

Second, I'm extremely good with analytics. I always provide alternatives for my clients and quantify them. In every situation, I use my experience to consider multiple possible real estate options. I prepare financial models unique to each client situation, summarizing the alternatives. I present each option with a net present value (NPV), a single number by which they can compare their potential choices. Presenting the numbers in an organized fashion and simplifying the decision assist tremendously in arriving at the right answer. My unique abilities help simplify the complex, and I make use of these strengths when coaching new agents, who of course benefit similarly later on. Although I consider myself a numbers guy and often use large spreadsheets, I'm able to convey messages in a very simple manner.

Throughout the thirty-five years of my professional life, I learned many important lessons. First, I learned to be eternally grateful for whatever happens in my life and to avoid getting upset if things don't go my way. I believe working hard is essential to create opportunities, but an equally important attitude involves gracefully accepting the results. Second, I realize that multiple paths lead to the top. We each need to choose our own path, and simultaneously understand we will face hurdles. The ability to view challenges as opportunities is crucial for ambitious humans. Finally, I regard humility as a fundamental key to professional success. The real estate business thrives on relationships, and clients choose to give business to those who are humble.

Real Estate Wisdom

The worth of all commercial properties relies on the underlying value of their leases. This concept serves not only as a fundamental truth, but also as the main differentiator between commercial and residential real estate. Commercial properties sell based primarily on the potential for future income from the real estate. By contrast, individuals selling their homes will work toward achieving the maximum price and will base pricing expectations on the amount that similar homes achieved when sold. Residential sales take historic trends into account, while commercial values focus more on future income potential.

Underlying leases seriously impact the value of property. Consider two identical properties, one with a short-term lease with a weak covenant tenant and another with a fifteen-year lease managed by a major Fortune 500 company. Clearly the property with greater potential for future income and lower risk of obtaining income of its own contains the most value.

Unfortunately, virtually all real estate licensing courses do not spend enough time on this essential subject matter. When new agents work on a form of offer to lease covering key business terms, they are expected to negotiate these points and send a signed agreement to lawyers who will help to secure the lease. An offer to lease, commonly referred to as a term sheet, typically spans one to three pages and simply cannot cover all of the relevant information from a 50- to 600-page lease. The disconnect between training of agents and the methodology of this process clearly presents a grave issue.

Real estate agents and commercial real estate lawyers take on two different roles in the ultimate signing of a lease agreement. Agents work "on the front lines," negotiating directly between tenants and landlords. They become very familiar with the space after walking the individual space, as well as the entire building, numerous times. Lawyers will often see the lease only one time, and then use their knowledge and expertise to ensure that the negotiated business terms and legal matters come together for the benefit and protection of their client.

The process for entering a new ten-year lease starts with a leasing mandate between the tenant and the real estate agent. The agent researches the market and provides the tenant with a number of realistic alternatives. Site tours help to identify a short-list, and subsequently offers to lease undergo negotiation one at a time until business terms are agreed upon by both landlord and tenant. The landlord then incorporates the signed offer to lease into a personal standard for lease, and this document makes its way to the tenant's lawyer. The lawyer reviews the document over a period of time and supplies comments and changes. Business changes must go through the agent for potential further negotiation.

An important tip: The tenant's agent should be certain that all issues reach resolution before going back to the landlord. Remember that a lease contains many clauses and that the agreement is not unlike a finely woven tapestry, becoming very difficult to negotiate or put back together one thread at a time. One should think of every clause as a poker chip and hold off on placing a bet until the whole picture is understood, in addition to what everyone else at the table holds. Agents must know the value of each chip, that is, the value of each clause in the offer to lease. Clauses with the same heading may not all consist of the same information. One renewal option will not simply work the same as another.

It is important for leasing professionals to identify possible lease clauses from both the tenant and landlord perspectives. Of course, I cannot share all possibilities and permutations. Instead, I provide two different, polar opposite perspectives. Each clause contains not only a definition, but also what agents should look out for, and a sample clause from a landlord and tenant perspective.

35 Years in Commercial Real Estate

Author's Bio

Hi – I am **Stephen Katz**. Your Commercial Real Agent at HomeLife Cimerman Commercial, soon to be known as HLC. Do you know anyone that owns a business that is growing, shrinking or changing? Do you know anyone who needs help with their lease or real estate decisions?

The typical problem most tenants face is that the Landlord has a huge advantage in the negotiating process.

They know their building and the real estate market much better than the tenant. They also know that it is time consuming, disruptive and expensive for the tenant to find space elsewhere. Landlords also leverage their relationship with the tenants to have them stay in the building and will convince the tenants that it is not in their best interest to hire a commercial real estate agent.

How do I know this? I used to be a landlord. The first rule of negotiating is to understand the other side's perspective. By hiring me you get someone in your corner with thirty-five years of commercial real estate experience and market knowledge, and you let the landlord know you are seriously considering your alternatives.

I am confident introducing me into the process will save you money. My promise is that if I can't save you money then I don't want to be paid. The tenant gets expert advice and I get paid by the landlord. It is a Win-Win-Win situation.

Please bring me your real estate questions.

Stephen Katz – HLC Commercial
"Simplifying the Complex"

"A Realtor with Extremely Loyal Clients"

Hamidreza Saeedabadi

Hamidreza Saeedabadi

Real Estate Agent

It is another Saturday morning and he is calling me on the phone, just as he has every single Saturday for the past six years. He always says the same thing when he calls. No, it's not annoying for me. I actually look forward to this call. This is a call from a happy client whom I was blessed to serve six years ago. And he tells me the same thing on every call: "You changed my life, Hamid. Thank you."

The first time this particular client called me was at 5:00 pm on a weekday. He said he had seen my post on my Facebook page, where I share useful content about the Toronto real estate market. He loved the energy in my photo and decided to reach out to me. He wanted to buy a property and to meet with me that very night. He was also truthful, telling me he had called three other agents who couldn't meet with him on such short notice.

I got curious and agreed to meet with him at my office within the hour. When I arrived, he was sitting at a table with his wife and his 3 kids. The story he then shared shook me to the core. A short while before, he had been scammed out of all the money he saved over the past few years. He told me he was not in a great financial situation, and he was sick of these circumstances. He was working very hard, and his wife was unemployed. To make things worse, he told me he was also in a lot of debt.

I asked him, "OK, what do you want to do?"

He replied, "Right now, we're renting a condo. We'd like to buy a property."

I asked him, "How much money do you have for the down payment?"

By his response I understood that it was going to be a challenging situation.

Then he asked, "Do you think we can buy a property?"

I answered, "It's definitely not going to be an easy thing to do. But if there's anybody in this town who can help you do it, that would be me."

I had the utmost empathy with the couple. There are peaks and valleys in any person's life, and this couple was at the lowest point in one of the deepest valleys. They were stressed-out and exhausted, had been hoodwinked out of their savings, and they just wanted to find a way to get back on track. I went to work for them immediately.

What I did for this couple over the following few weeks was nothing short of a miracle. I utilized my network to get the wife a job. I also introduced a couple of mortgage specialists for them to choose from to help them get a mortgage. After a while they were able to secure mortgage pre-approval, and after a few days of hard work I finally found them a great property in a prime location. I further negotiated a wonderful price with the seller's realtor. I did everything in my power to help their family climb out of the low spot in which they had found themselves.

When we closed the deal—a very long and complicated process, I was "over the moon" because I had managed to do the impossible. This is why the client has called me every single Saturday since the successful conclusion to express his gratitude.

My Bitter Experience

Unlike the happy story you read above, I personally had a very bitter experience in real estate after I came to Canada as a new immigrant. Immediately after I landed,

I started actively looking for a property to buy, because I didn't want my money to be parked in the bank and lose value over time. I knew if I put my money into real estate, I would protect its value in the long run. I was then introduced to a family friend in Toronto, a realtor that helped me find and purchase a house within only ten days of being in Canada. Things moved so fast; that was how long it took before I applied for the title transfer.

That deal closed smoothly, and I became the owner of a very good property in a great location. Since I was happy with my purchase, over the next few months, I introduced my realtor to a few other friends and family members who wanted to buy and sell their properties. Unfortunately, those transactions did not go well, which I only realized later on.

 A few weeks after purchasing my property, the realtor called me and let me know about a real estate investment opportunity. He said, "There are a couple of condos in a pre-construction project in a very good location in the city. You can buy them and later assign them to other buyers, whenever you wish, at a higher price, or if you can't find a buyer then, I'll buy them from you myself and give you $10,000 profit on your purchase price for each one you buy. This is a very good opportunity that I don't want you to miss."

Because of the trust I placed in him, I said, "If you say so, I believe you. Let's do it." Soon afterwards, I made the deposit for the condo and asked the agent to keep me in the loop as to what the next steps would be.

A few weeks later, I received a letter from the developer saying that the unit would be ready for occupancy in a month. I was startled to receive that letter because I wasn't expecting the news so soon, since the realtor told me the unit would be ready by the end of the following year, not at the beginning of the current year. Besides, I thought the realtor would give me fair warning, well in advance, so I could get prepared for the next steps, and he hadn't. Since my intention at the time was to dedicate my financial assets toward a business I was going to start, I didn't want to close on the condo. With that being said, I called the realtor and told him I didn't want to close the deal and reminded him of the promise he made.

"I didn't say that. What do you think I am, crazy?" he replied.

I was shocked. I said, "This is exactly what you told me

when you first contacted me. You said that you would assign the condo for me at a profit or you'd buy it from me yourself." He denied having said that. "Then, what do I do now?" I asked.

He said, "Go close your purchase. Sit on it for a while and sell it at a good profit later on."

At that moment, I felt paralyzed and betrayed. I had trusted this man's word and he had taken advantage of me. I now had to use all my nest egg and every single penny in my bank account to close the deal, which put me in a very insecure position as a new immigrant who did not have a steady stream of income yet. I soon learned that not only was the building in a very poor location and a bad investment altogether, but I also had no right to assign the unit to anyone else, based on the agreement of purchase and sale. This news shocked me even more. Gratefully, I had the connections to help me secure a mortgage for the unit and eventually to close the deal on time. Nonetheless, that experience left me strained emotionally and financially.

Since I was unhappy with my purchase this time, I decided to sell it right away so that I could have cash on hand to focus on my idea of starting a business in Canada. That was why I asked another realtor to help me sell the property.

The new realtor turned out to be someone who was just after his commission and didn't really care about the client, in my opinion. In just a few hours, he listed the condo with a sale price well below the average of comparable properties on the market at that time. He didn't take any of the standard steps that would be expected of a listing agent: doing market research, getting an appraisal, having a marketing plan, advertising, and so on. He also clearly didn't address my concerns. I eventually sold the unit and came out of the situation with a hefty loss, nearly $40k, and months of headache. This felt like a double insult for someone like me, who is super-organized, attentive to detail, and purely ethical.

Lessons Learned

I learned a lot from that sad experience and grew wiser in the process. I realized how important it is to have a reliable realtor when you are making one of the biggest and most important transactions in your life. I had been mistreated twice by two different agents, both of whom betrayed my trust so they could profit.

Yes, money is important, and one must have it in order to enjoy a high standard of living, but money is in no way the most important thing in the world. For me, people always come first. In any business relationship, I put people first, because relationships are much more important to me than the financial transaction. And maybe that's why 90% of my current business comes from referrals from happy clients.

I also realized that any client would want their realtor to care, to take the time and effort to educate them and keep them informed all along the way. I explain every single line of all agreements and standard forms to my clients, taking time to explain my duties and responsibilities to them.

I obey the Code of Ethics. I never rush clients into making a decision so I can get my commission faster. I believe any good realtor must follow the Golden Rule: Treat your clients just like you want to be treated. I see it as a privilege to share some of the most joyful moments of my clients' lives with them, especially when they are buying a property and particularly if they're new immigrants. There's seldom anything so beautiful and heartwarming as seeing a family step into the house where they will build beautiful memories and that is what makes me love my job.

Undecided Which Way to Go

After I got over my initial real estate trauma, it was time to decide what I wanted to do professionally as a new immigrant. I knew I was never meant to be someone else's employee, and I intended to be in the business world, as I had all my life. I considered several options going forward.

First, I could go back to the industry I was familiar with before immigrating: telecom and computers. I had a software engineering degree and the experience of building a very successful telecom franchise business; however, it was one thing to succeed back home where most of my competitors were very small independent businesses and another thing entirely in North America, where I would have to compete against giant corporations such as Bell, Rogers, Best Buy and so on.

My second alternative was to buy a franchise, which

I explored very carefully. None of the options I came across in my research fit my background, expertise and passions. For example, there were lots of possibilities in the food or high-tech industries which didn't match my profile in the least.

My third choice was to start an international business to import and export goods. I had years of experience in that area, too.

Seeing that none of these three was the optimum solution for me, I continued my research to find other viable pathways where I could start my professional trajectory in Canada. Given the very impactful experiences I had under my belt, I decided to get licensed as a realtor and take complete control of the process. I thought, "If I become licensed, I can at least take care of my own buying and selling and be knowledgeable in this matter."

Baby Steps in Real Estate

Having made that conscious choice, I signed up for licensing courses at the Ontario Real Estate College and, with dedicated focus, I managed to graduate from the program with straight A's in all my courses.

After graduation, I had no clients, but I wanted to get really good at my craft. I decided to write hypothetical offers to see how prepared I actually was to help a client. I sat down in the office, pulled up Multiple Listing Service (MLS), opened up an offer document on my computer, and began to write an imaginary offer for that property. Immediately, I was stuck. Yes, I had learned my stuff very well in college, and I knew everything that was to be done theoretically; however, the real-life process was absolutely different. I needed to know how and where to use the knowledge I had learned in my courses. Although I had passed my exams with flying colors, I wasn't ready to take on real clients yet.

This realization led me to do something very unique. Every single day for the following few months, I wrote hypothetical offers for listings on MLS, acting both as a buyer's and as a seller's realtor. Whenever I got bogged down, I asked my office managers and more experienced colleagues at the brokerage for help. I even worked on made-up situations, such as multi-offers. I also used every single resource that was available to help me boost my knowledge and expertise: the Toronto Regional Real Estate Board. RECO, CREA, my books and pamphlets from college, and many others.

Overall, I wrote many many imaginary offers during those first few months, which helped me become extremely confident in my skill set. I still have the box where all those imaginary offers are stored, and I sometimes look at it to remind me how I started out in the real estate world.

I made my first transaction a few months after becoming registered as a realtor. A friend asked me to represent him while he bought a property. Given all the practice I had gained, I wrote the offer, and thankfully it was accepted right away without a single glitch. This made me even more self-assured.

Things started moving at a relatively fast pace after that initial deal. The people in my network (mostly friends and family members) became aware of what I was doing and gradually began to trust me with their realty transactions. After doing a transaction for another friend, I realized I already had a few transactions to my credit and a successful beginning of my real estate career.

Fork in the Road

Although I was happy to be trusted as a realtor by family and friends, I began to doubt if real estate was truly the right thing for me. I recognized the internal chatter I'd been having for quite a while. "My current income this year covered only one fifth of my family expenses. How am I supposed to make this work over the long term? What if real estate is not a reliable source of income? Maybe I should look for other opportunities as well. What other opportunities? I have looked at all of them. Telecom, franchise, import and export. None works for me. What should I do?"

Disappointing as it was to recognize these thoughts, I began to talk back to them, "Hamid! Of course, you can make this work. You've started from scratch twice before and built two big empires. You were the one who went into a manufacturing company in cable industries (the leader of the cable industry in the country) and grew one of their divisions from smaller scale activities to a well-known and successful business in sales within just a few years. You were the one who started your own business and grew it to a reputable telecom franchise back home.

You did each of those when you were younger and less experienced than your present self."

All of that mind chatter was true. I knew I was persistent. I knew I had the necessary stick-to-it-ness to turn everything in my favor. Many years prior to this, I tried to get my company on the vendor list of a very large division of a huge and influential company. I went to their head office and requested a meeting with the procurement department to submit a proposal. The security officer of their building didn't allow me to meet the decision makers. He said, "Oh no, you can't go in without THEM wanting to see you first."

The next day, I showed up again. The security officer said, "Why are you here again? I told you yesterday you can't go in."

I replied, "I just want five minutes of their time. I have everything ready, and I won't take long."

He didn't let me in. I kept going to that building and showed up at the security guard's window every single day for the next two weeks. Eventually, he gave in and allowed me to enter after two weeks of dogged persistence. I managed to get my company name on their vendor list, and over time, they became one of our biggest clients, making lots of orders every year. Persistence pays off, always.

That was why I decided to stay in my realty role. I said to myself, "I'm going to make this work, big time. In a few short years, I will be a type of Realtor who everyone would like to work with."

I didn't give up. I kept pushing. I utilized my network, did a lot of marketing, and provided exemplary service to my clients. And slowly, my client base grew. My income grew. So did my success.

A Decade in Real Estate

I have been a full-time realtor for the past few years. I now handle residential and commercial real estate and have a large base of clients, some of whom are investors and builders that trust me and my advice. I'm overjoyed to have the most loyal clientele in the world and to be friends with a number of my clients.

I attribute my success in real estate to five main character traits:

1. Honesty. That's my number one. As a real estate representative, I will always protect my clients' interests while considering their needs and priorities. I believe it is my responsibility to provide the facts and details to my clients.

2. Integrity. The real estate market is very competitive, and it is extremely important to follow and obey the Code of Ethics. I never do business "at any price." Integrity and honesty always come first for me. They have direct and indirect effects and are beneficial to all aspects of a real estate transaction.

3. Knowledge. Even after so many years in business, I study every day. I devour websites, listen to podcasts and interviews of seasoned real estate experts, go to seminars and courses regularly, and use all the tools and resources I can access.

4. Experience. It's always great to know your stuff theoretically. But practical real-world experience takes you to another level. An experienced realtor is like a guide in a jungle that

helps you navigate the unknown paths. Experience, combined with honesty and knowledge, is the holy grail for success in real estate.

5. Organization. I have always been extremely organized and very good at planning. Years ago, I was a team member in implementing a series of ISO 9000 standards in a cable industry company. I was trained extensively for that role and have used that skill set ever since. Everything in my business follows a standard, has a form which comes with a checklist, and is documented. I even designed uniquely exclusive forms to guide and improve the quality of my service to my clients. These procedures, as well as the standard forms and documentation, help me more effectively understand the needs and priorities of every single client, while I also stay organized and attentive to details.

Over the course of these many years, I gained the privilege to access a group of professionals in my network that can help my clients with all their needs in real estate.

I'm just a realtor, and I always recommend my clients obtain appropriate advice from professional, licensed, and reliable experts, such as lawyers, mortgage brokers, accountants, inspectors, etc., to help them achieve their goals. I serve my clients in every way possible, and I urge them to seek legal and technical advice from other experts whenever they are in a high-stakes situation.

My goal for the future is to go beyond the Greater Toronto Area and lead a team of realtors all over Ontario.

Now let me give you some tips based on my experience to make the process of buying and selling easier.

Tips for sellers

- Hire an experienced and knowledgeable Realtor.
- Set the right price.
- Take care of home landscape.
- Clear out all the non-essentials.
- Paint your interior if need be.
- Consider a professional cleaning.
- Insist on professional photography.
- Use a Virtual Tour.

- Smell is powerful: avoid bad odors.
- Take your pets somewhere for the times of showing.
- Keep the house organized.
- Be flexible with home showings.
- Prepare for closing and moving.

Tips for buyers

- Make sure you have secured your down payment.
- Hire an experienced and knowledgeable Realtor.
- Determine what you can afford.
- Budget for closing costs.
- Save enough for after move-in expenses.
- Explore mortgage options and rates.
- Get a mortgage preapproval letter.
- Choose the type of home that meets your needs.
- Pick the right neighborhood.
- Stick to your budget when you make an offer.
- Do a home inspection.
- Buy adequate homeowner's insurance.
- Prepare for closing and moving.

*A Realtor
with Extremely
Loyal Clients*

Author's Bio

Hamidreza Saeedabadi

is a successful, fulltime realtor who is a member of Toronto Regional Real Estate Board and has long years of experience in assisting clients with their residential and commercial needs in Greater Toronto Area (GTA). He is well connected and actively involved in the community and is highly regarded by his clients and other professionals in the field.

His honesty, integrity, and organizational skills have

helped him to build a business through referral from past clients, friends, and industry contacts, which has resulted in establishing a strong base of loyal repeat clients in an incredibly competitive field. Not to mention that his knowledge and education in engineering and management have also been a great asset in terms of paying attention to details, using appropriate research methods, and critically assessing the situation to be able to achieve the desired outcomes for the clients.

Aside from his work ethic, Hamidreza is a caring family guy who loves his family. In addition, it is always his interest to support his family and friends, not to mention new immigrants who are struggling with the new challenges especially in Real Estate matters. His hobbies include playing and watching soccer, spending time with his family, watching movies and most importantly being involved in social activities that help and support the environment.

Hamidreza's unique characteristics in both personal and work life have made him become the person he is today and have helped him significantly to become successful in this field. He celebrated this success in 2019 by being featured in Star Metro Toronto newspaper as a business owner with prominent success in Canada after long years of hard work and experience and being one of the top Realtors over the past few years in Greater Toronto Area (GTA). However, he believes that his most rewarding accomplishment has been to achieve a high client satisfaction rate. This high satisfaction rate is achieved when clients receive Hamidreza's full support from beginning to end.

When providing his services, Hamidreza works with a group of experienced professionals in his network that can help his clients with all their needs in real estate. He shares his network of professional, licensed, and reliable high-quality experts who are able to assist his clients in achieving in their desired goals in Real Estate transactions.

He works with all communities for all their residential and commercial needs and Real Estate transactions. One of Hamidreza's areas of expertise is to provide a wide range of services for newcomers and first-time home buyers. Hamidreza also serves some of the Greater Toronto Area's most influential individuals, developers, and companies. He believes that his role is to help people make the right decisions for a better future.